CONNER'S EZ-PASS 220-902

GET COMPTIA A+ CERTIFIED

CompTIA's 220-902 Q & A Study Guide

Dive deep into the 220-902 exam with our Q & A Study-Guide that guarantees you pass! We provide the exact questions, answers, and explainations as needed to pass this exam makeup of Windows, iOS, Android, OS X and Linux

C.V. Conner, Ph.D.
#1 Bestselling author of 'A+ In 21 Days - 2009

Get CompTIA A+ Certified

In 21 Days with Conner's EZ-Pass for Exam 220-902

Dive deep into the 220-902 exam now with our Q & A Study guide that guarantees you pass! We've provided the exact questions, answers, and explainations as we believe is necessary to pass the 220-902 exam with it's makeup of primarily software, but extending to coverage of the operating systems like Windows, Mac, and Linux.

© **Copyright 2016 by C.V.Conner - All rights reserved.**

This document is geared towards providing exact and reliable information in regards to the topic and issue covered. The publication is sold with the idea that the publisher is not required to render accounting, officially permitted, or otherwise, qualified services. If advice is necessary, legal or professional, a practiced individual in the profession should be ordered.

[From a Declaration of Principles which was accepted and approved equally by a Committee of the American Bar Association and a Committee of Publishers and Associations.]

In no way is it legal to reproduce, duplicate, or transmit any part of this document in either electronic means or in printed format. Recording of this publication is strictly prohibited and any storage of this document is not allowed unless with written permission from the publisher. All rights reserved.

The information provided herein is stated to be truthful and consistent, in that any liability, in terms of inattention or otherwise, by any usage or abuse of any policies, processes, or directions contained within is the solitary and utter responsibility of the recipient reader. Under no circumstances will any legal responsibility or blame be held against the publisher for any reparation, damages, or monetary loss due to the information herein, either directly or indirectly.

The respective author own all copyrights not held by the publisher.

The information herein is offered for educational informational purposes solely, and is universal as so. The presentation of the information is without contract or any type of guarantee assurance.

The trademarks that are used are without any consent, and the publication of the trademark is without permission or backing by the trademark owner. All trademarks and brands within this book are for clarifying purposes only and are owned by the owners themselves, not affiliated with this document.

ISBN: 978-1-365-29368-9

Introduction

Thank you for downloading the book, *"Comptia A+ In 21 Days Study Guide 220-902"*. The fact you've taken an interest in computer repairs and/or networking means you're already aware of the power that this certification can bring to your life and career. That's half the battle. Now all you need is a few hours to start building your career muscles, studying this powerful and easy to remember study guide that will help you to pass your exam quickly!

This book contains proven steps, questions, answers, and explanations where needed about how to govern your time, and memorize your way to certification. You'll find out the exact questions to be looking out for. And you'll also be given the incredible opportunity to prepare yourself completely from the comforts of your own home.

Hundreds of people will attempt to complete a traditional college course for CompTIA A+ this year. Many of them will fail the class. And many more will not be able to successfully pass the certification exams without the assistance of a book just like this one, even after completing the year long program. What that means is that you will be way ahead of the others by bypassing the traditional route and using this book to gain your certification quickly. So if you are planning to start a new career in computers, or if you already have one, it's essential to use this type of book to complete your certifications and save thousands of dollars in the process.

This book will prevent you from spending too much time using trial-and-error methods. It will save you hundreds if not thousands of dollars, and it will provide you with tested methods to make sure you're successful without having taken any prior computer classes! Thanks again for downloading this book!

Right before we get into the actual study guide, allow me to explain a couple of things that you may want to be aware of.

First off, CompTIA has made a few major changes in these latest exams from the 220-800 series exams. The CompTIA 220-900 series exams include both some changes that we was expecting, and some that came as a bit of a surprise.

If for whatever reason you had started to study but got side-tracked, or you just knew a bit about those 800 series exams, then this exam should look pretty familiar to you. I'd estimate that about 75% of the new exam objectives are identical to the previous version. But, some of the older technologies have been replaced, and some new topics have been added. Rambus, CRTs, and Windows XP have all been removed and Windows 8, Mac OS, Linux, and Windows Phone have taken their places.

In fact, the overall structure of the exams have been changed too to make each exam more self-contained. So unlike the 220-802 exam where they expected you to know all of the troubleshooting processes for every topic across both exams, the 220-901 and the 220-902 now have their own individual troubleshooting domains. What that means is that you can now focus your study efforts on passing a single exam before putting all those materials away and starting on the next exam. This is a big and very helpful change to every student's study plans.

To stay abreast of these new format changes I have written all my 900 series study guides and the training manuals in a way that better accommodates the new layouts. For example, instead of producing one bulky training manual I have broken my material down so that you can now get a lighter or thinner Training Manual & the Study guide for exam 220-901. That way you only have to deal with the materials that apply specifically to the 220-901 exam. After you have passed that exam, you can return and get the 220-902 Training Manual & the 22-902 Study guide. If you're familiar with my past books then you know that I'm a big believer in memorization. And I believe that this new format from both Comptia and myself is going to make getting your certification a lot easier and a lot faster! So with that being said, lets just dive right in now to the Q & A section. Know it, memorize it, pass with it. It's just that easy.

Comptia A+ In 21 Days 220-902 Study Guide

By: C.V.Conner

Released Date: 7/27/16

QUESTION 1

A customer with a PC has requested assistance setting up Windows 7 parental controls within the web browser. The customer would like to limit how much time a
child can spend on a particular website. Which of the following tabs under Internet Options will allow the user to create those settings?
A. Privacy
B. Advanced
C. Security
D. Content
Correct Answer: D
Section: Windows Operating System
Explanation
Explanation/Reference:

QUESTION 2

A technician is performing a clean install of Windows on a new hard drive from a factory DVD, but the computer does not recognize the optical disc. A "non-system
disk or disk error" is observed. Which of the following should the technician do FIRST?
A. Update the motherboard firmware
B. Check the cables
C. Replace the optical drive

D. Check the BIOS setting
Correct Answer: D
Section: Windows Operating System
Explanation
Explanation/Reference:

QUESTION 3

An administrator has a new workstation that has been loaded with the Windows OS and configured with the proper IP settings. The workstation needs to be added
to the corporation's domain. Which of the following utilities will the administrator access to configure this setting?
A. System Properties
B. System Information
C. System Protection
D. System Management
Correct Answer: A
Section: Windows Operating System
Explanation
Explanation/Reference:

QUESTION 4

A technician is attempting to remove malware from a customer's workstation. Which of the following Control Panel utilities should the technician use?
A. Folder Options > View hidden files
B. System > Performance
C. Display Settings > Refresh rate
D. Internet Options > Privacy
Correct Answer: A
Section: Windows Operating System

Explanation
Explanation/Reference:

QUESTION 5

Which of the following should be used to ensure that a Windows OS is functioning optimally?
A. Driver updates
B. Scheduled backups
C. Application updates
D. Restore points
Correct Answer: A
Section: Windows Operating System
Explanation
Explanation/Reference:

QUESTION 6

A technician needs to log into a user's computer to fix the user's corrupt local profile. Which of the following connectivity tools will allow the technician to connect to
the user's computer?
A. Remote Assistance
B. Virtual Private Network
C. Computer Management
D. Remote Desktop
Correct Answer: D
Section: Windows Operating System
Explanation
Explanation/Reference:

QUESTION 7

An end user needs to completely re-install Windows 7 on a home computer but it did not come with any OS discs. How would a technician accomplish this?
A. Recovery partition
B. Primary partition
C. System restore
D. System refresh
Correct Answer: A
Section: Windows Operating System
Explanation
Explanation/Reference:

QUESTION 8

A user is unable to find the preferred default network printer in the printers list in the user profile. Which of the following is the FIRST step that should be taken?
A. Map printer
B. Reboot computer
C. Check to see if printer is turned on
D. Log in as a different user and see if printer is mapped
Correct Answer: A
Section: Windows Operating System
Explanation
Explanation/Reference:

QUESTION 9

A technician needs to perform a backup while a system is running. Which of the following services allows this task to be accomplished?
A. Robocopy
B. Shadow copy

C. Xcopy
D. System restore
Correct Answer: B
Section: Windows Operating System
Explanation
Explanation/Reference:

QUESTION 10

A technician has been tasked with loading the operating system on every PC with a blank hard drive on a network. The technician wishes to install the operating
system with minimal physical interaction with the PCs. Which of the following is the BEST way to accomplish this?
A. Clone the operating system from an image onto optical media.
B. Use the original software media to load the operation system on every PC.
C. Set up a central image that the PCs can load from a PXE boot.
D. Create an image and copy it from a USB drive using an unattended answer file.
Correct Answer: C
Section: Windows Operating System
Explanation
Explanation/Reference:

QUESTION 11

A technician is navigating through a Windows OS via command prompt. The technician needs to display the content of a folder. Which of the following is the BEST
option for accomplishing this task?
A. dir
B. ls

C. rd
D. cmd
Correct Answer: A
Section: Windows Operating System
Explanation
Explanation/Reference:

QUESTION 12

A network administrator needs to connect to resources from an offsite location while ensuring the traffic is protected. Which of the following should the administrator use to gain access to the secure network?
A. SSH
B. VPN
C. SFTP
D. RDP
Correct Answer: B
Section: Windows Operating System
Explanation
Explanation/Reference:

QUESTION 13

A user states that when typing in directions on a navigation website, the map is not viewable in a newer web browser. The technician runs updates to Java, but is still unable to view the map. The technician should change which of the following Internet Options?
A. Compatibility view
B. Manage add-ons
C. Clear browser cache
D. Pop-up blocker
Correct Answer: A
Section: Windows Operating System

Explanation
Explanation/Reference:

QUESTION 14

A technician has successfully completed a gpupdate from a CMD box of a user's PC and is ready to move to the next user. Which of the following is the appropriate NEXT step? (Select TWO).
A. View the CMD process in Task Manager
B. Type EXIT at the command prompt and press Enter
C. Minimize the CMD box to the taskbar
D. Click the "x" in the top right of the CMD window
E. Select Switch User on the PC
Correct Answer: BD
Section: Windows Operating System
Explanation
Explanation/Reference:

QUESTION 15
An administrator is in a Remote Assistance session, sharing a user's desktop. While trying to map a shared network drive for the user, an "access denied" error is encountered while using the user's credentials. Which of the following should be the administrator's NEXT step?
A. Ensure the user's account is not locked out
B. Use the fully qualified domain name of the share
C. Open the location with administrator privileges
D. Try mapping with a different drive letter
Correct Answer: C
Section: Windows Operating System
Explanation
Explanation/Reference:

QUESTION 16

Ann, a user, discovers that all of her documents will not open. The documents open properly on another computer. Which of the following tools will be the FASTEST for a technician to use to allow the documents to open?
A. Backup
B. Recovery Image
C. chkdsk
D. System Restore
Correct Answer: D
Section: Windows Operating System
Explanation
Explanation/Reference:

QUESTION 17
A technician is tasked with enabling TLS version 1.0, 1.1, and 1.2 on a client Internet Explorer browser. Which of the following Internet Options Tabs should the
technician look to enable the aforementioned TLS settings?
A. Advanced
B. Security
C. Privacy
D. Connections
Correct Answer: A
Section: Windows Operating System
Explanation
Explanation/Reference:

QUESTION 18
Which of the following network hosts would MOST likely provide the services needed to allow client access to Internet web pages?
A. File server
B. Web server
C. WINS server

D. Proxy server
Correct Answer: D
Section: Other
Explanation
Explanation/Reference:

QUESTION 19
Which of the following best practices is used to fix a zero-day vulnerability on Linux?
A. Scheduled backup
B. Scheduled disk maintenance
C. Patch management
D. Antivirus update
Correct Answer: C
Section: Other
Explanation
Explanation/Reference:

QUESTION 20
Which of the following tools is used to type or paste recovery commands directly into a Linux box?
A. Shell/terminal
B. Backup/time machine
C. Command/cmd
D. Restore/snapshot
Correct Answer: A
Section: Other
Explanation
Explanation/Reference:

QUESTION 21
A technician is installing Bluetooth speakers in a conference room. Which of the following will be the average operating range of the

speakers?
A. 10 feet (3 meters)
B. 15 feet (5 meters)
C. 30 feet (9 meters)
D. 45 feet (14 meters)
Correct Answer: C
Section: Other
Explanation
Explanation/Reference:

QUESTION 22
A user has a Windows 8.1 RT operating system and wants to add additional programs to the computer. Which of the following is available for installing more applications?
A. Microsoft Store
B. DVD
C. Google Play
D. iTunes
Correct Answer: A
Section: Other
Explanation
Explanation/Reference:

QUESTION 23
A company that manages its own cloud, while utilizing a third-party vendor to help manage storage, is implementing which of the following infrastructure types?
A. Hybrid
B. Community
C. Private
D. Public
Correct Answer: A
Section: Other

Explanation
Explanation/Reference:

QUESTION 24
An administrator has a virtual client running but cannot receive network connectivity. The host workstation is able to access the network. Which of the following would the administrator check on the host to repair the problem?
A. The cable connected to the network
B. Virtual host network adapter
C. USB host adapter
D. The domain of the virtual machine
Correct Answer: B
Section:
Explanation
Explanation/Reference:

QUESTION 25
A Google account on an Android device by default will synchronize to which of the following locations?
A. Cloud
B. SSD
C. PC desktop
D. MicroSD
Correct Answer: A
Section: Other
Explanation
Explanation/Reference:

QUESTION 26
How would a technician install Windows OS on a MAC OS computer without using third-party software?
A. Terminal

B. Boot Disk
C. Disk Utility
D. Boot Camp
Correct Answer: D
Section: Other
Explanation
Explanation/Reference:

QUESTION 27
A user wants to configure a smartphone to save all attachments from an Outlook.com email to a cloud-based service. Which of the following would be BEST to use to accomplish this?
A. Google Drive
B. iCloud
C. One Drive
D. FTP
Correct Answer: C
Section: Other
Explanation
Explanation/Reference:

QUESTION 28
Virtual machines provide users with the ability to do which of the following?
A. Extend 32-bit machines to 64-bits
B. Share hardware resources
C. Increase the network download speed
D. Use less memory in the machine
Correct Answer: B
Section: Other
Explanation
Explanation/Reference:

QUESTION 29
Which of the following features of a mobile device operates the touch screen?
A. Gyroscope
B. Digitizer
C. Accelerometer
D. Geotracking
Correct Answer: B
Section: Other
Explanation
Explanation/Reference:

QUESTION 30
A technician contacts the network administrator to request a list of all static IP addresses in the building. Which of the following server roles would the technician MOST likely review to find that information?
A. DHCP server
B. DNS server
C. File server
D. Proxy server
Correct Answer: A
Section: Other
Explanation
Explanation/Reference:

QUESTION 31
A technician is tasked with setting up a user's webmail on a tablet, phone, and laptop. The user would like the data synced to all three devices. Which of the following items can be synced to the devices via webmail? (Select THREE).
A. Free/busy
B. Programs

C. Documents
D. Calendar
E. Favorites
F. Social media
G. Contacts
Correct Answer: ADG
Section: Other
Explanation
Explanation/Reference:

QUESTION 32
A network administrator is unable to install programs on a workstation. Which of the following is MOST likely the reason the administrator is not able to install applications?
A. The workstation is victim of a denial of service attack.
B. The username is not authenticating on the network.
C. The username is not part of the local administrator group.
D. The administrator has not applied appropriate security patches.
Correct Answer: C
Section: Security
Explanation
Explanation/Reference:

QUESTION 33
A technician has been tasked with limiting the users who can connect to a network printer located centrally within an office environment. Which of the following tools would be the BEST to utilize to achieve this goal?
A. VPN
B. ACL
C. RDP
D. DLP
Correct Answer: B

Section: Security
Explanation
Explanation/Reference:

QUESTION 34
An end user has reported not receiving emails sent by a specific customer. Which of the following is the MOST likely cause of this issue?
A. The HIPS device is blocking the messages
B. The access control list is blocking the messages
C. The email filter has quarantined the messages
D. The firewall is blocking the sender's email address
Correct Answer: C
Section: Security
Explanation
Explanation/Reference:

QUESTION 35
A new user reports trying to login to a workstation but, when pressing CTRL+ALT+DEL, they are asked for a PIN. Which of the following should be done NEXT?
A. Enter all passwords they have used in the past
B. Verify a smart card has been issued
C. Check the network cable
D. Reboot the computer
Correct Answer: B
Section: Security
Explanation
Explanation/Reference:

QUESTION 36
A user, Ann, has reported that she lost a laptop. The laptop had sensitive corporate information on it that has been published on the Internet. Which of the following is the FIRST step in implementing a

best practice security policy?
A. Require biometric identification to log into the laptop.
B. Require multifactor authentication to log into laptop.
C. Require laptop hard drives to be encrypted.
D. Require users to change their password at frequent intervals.
E. Require users to have strong passwords.
Correct Answer: C
Section: Security
Explanation
Explanation/Reference:

QUESTION 37
The type of security threat that uses computers or other networks to accept and pass on viruses is called:
A. phishing.
B. botnets.
C. logic bomb.
D. man-in-the-middle.
Correct Answer: B
Section: Security
Explanation
Explanation/Reference:

QUESTION 38
Joe, a user, just downloaded a game onto his company phone. When he is not using the device, it unexpectedly dials unrecognized numbers and downloads new content. Joe is the victim of which of the following?
A. Trojan horse
B. Spyware
C. Social engineering
D. Worms
Correct Answer: A
Section: Security

Explanation
Explanation/Reference:

QUESTION 39
A technician is attempting to manually migrate a user's profile from one Windows PC to another. Files in the user's My Documents folder cannot be copied. Some files in question have green letters in the filenames. Which of the following file systems is causing this to occur?
A. exFAT
B. COMPRESSED
C. EFS
D. NTFS
Correct Answer: C
Section: Security
Explanation
Explanation/Reference:

QUESTION 40

When securing a mobile device, which of the following types of screen locks is the MOST secure?
A. Fingerprint lock
B. Swipe lock
C. Passcode lock
D. Face lock
Correct Answer: A
Section: Security
Explanation
Explanation/Reference:

QUESTION 41
A technician has upgraded four computers and would like to securely repurpose the hard drives for later use. Which of the following should

the technician do to the drives to prepare them for later use?
A. chkdsk
B. Degauss
C. Quick format
D. Drive wipe
Correct Answer: D
Section: Security
Explanation
Explanation/Reference:

QUESTION 42
A technician is configuring a SOHO wireless router for a small business with three employees. After the three employees' laptops have successfully connected to the wireless network, the company would like to prevent additional access to the wireless network. The technician enables WPA2 on the wireless router. Which of the following additional settings should the technician change?
A. Enable MAC filtering
B. Disable SSID broadcast
C. Reduce radio power level
D. Update router firmware
Correct Answer: A
Section: Security
Explanation
Explanation/Reference:

QUESTION 43
A technician is configuring wireless for a home office. The customer wants to prevent others from accessing the wireless network. The customer has a small number of devices on the network and does not want to have to remember a complicated password. Which of the following should the technician recommend?
A. Enable MAC filtering

B. Disable SSID broadcast
C. Assign static IP addresses
D. Turn on content filtering
Correct Answer: A
Section: Security
Explanation
Explanation/Reference:

QUESTION 44
A technician has been notified that recent vulnerabilities have been discovered related to a type of SOHO router. The technician has verified that all connections and settings are appropriate. Which of the following actions should the technician take NEXT?
A. Change the router firewall settings
B. Check for and apply a firmware update
C. Reconfigure the QoS settings
D. Change router user-names and passwords
Correct Answer: B
Section: Security
Explanation
Explanation/Reference:

QUESTION 45
A technician needs to quickly destroy data on several hard drives that are no longer wanted. Which of the following methods is MOST effective?
A. Physical destruction
B. Quick format
C. Low level format
D. Overwrite
Correct Answer: A
Section: Security

Explanation
Explanation/Reference:

QUESTION 46
Which of the following will help to protect an organization from further data exposure AFTER a list of user passwords has already been leaked due to policy breach? (Select TWO).
A. Use multi-factor authentication
B. Require strong passwords
C. Enable file encryption
D. Educate end users
E. Restrict user permissions
Correct Answer: AD
Section: Security
Explanation
Explanation/Reference:

QUESTION 47
A technician has been tasked with disposing of hard drives that contain sensitive employee data. Which of the following would be the BEST method to use for disposing of these drives?
A. Recycling
B. Shredding
C. Overwriting
D. Reformatting
Correct Answer: B
Section: Security
Explanation
Explanation/Reference:

QUESTION 48
Ann, an executive, reports that she received a call from someone asking for information about her email account. Which of the following type of

potential security threats does this scenario describe?
A. Social engineering
B. Spoofing
C. Zero-day
D. Man-in-the-middle
Correct Answer: A
Section: Security
Explanation
Explanation/Reference:

QUESTION 49
A technician is configuring a new Windows computer for a home office. Which of the following steps should the technician take to secure the workstation? (Select TWO).
A. Rename default accounts
B. Disable Windows Update
C. Configure single sign-on
D. Run gpupdate tool
E. Disable guest account
F. Disable Action Center pop-ups
Correct Answer: AE
Section: Security
Explanation
Explanation/Reference:

QUESTION 50
Which of the following prevention methods is considered to be digital security?
A. RFID badge
B. Mantrap
C. Biometrics
D. Firewalls
E. ID badge

Correct Answer: D
Section: Security
Explanation
Explanation/Reference:

QUESTION 51
Which of the following Windows features would be used to encrypt a single file or folder?
A. EFS
B. NTFS
C. BitLocker
D. Security
Correct Answer: A
Section: Security
Explanation
Explanation/Reference:

QUESTION 52
A turnstile is an example of which of the following forms of physical security?
A. Entry control roster
B. Biometrics
C. Mantrap
D. Cipher lock
Correct Answer: C
Section: Security
Explanation
Explanation/Reference:

QUESTION 53
A user wants to save a file into another user's directory, but the file save is denied. Which of the following is the MOST likely reason the file save cannot be completed?

A. The user must be a member of the Users group
B. The user requires write permissions to the folder
C. The user requires read permission to the folder
D. The user must be a member of the Administrators group
Correct Answer: B
Section: Security
Explanation
Explanation/Reference:

QUESTION 54
A user leaves the workstation frequently and does not want sensitive material to be accessed. In addition, the user does not want to turn off the computer every time in the evening. Which of the following is the BEST solution for securing the workstation?
A. Set a strong password that requires a renewal every 30 days.
B. Run a screensaver after one minute of nonuse and fingerprint lock for afterhours.
C. Apply a screen lock after five minutes of nonuse and login time restrictions for afterhours.
D. Require a password and fingerprint lock afterhours.
Correct Answer: C
Section: Security
Explanation
Explanation/Reference:

QUESTION 55
A technician is configuring a SOHO router to ensure network computers can only use secured protocols on the Internet. Which of the following ports should be allowed?
A. 143
B. 23
C. 443
D. 3269

E. 3389
Correct Answer: C
Section: Security
Explanation
Explanation/Reference:

QUESTION 56
An end-user is attempting to access a file-sharing site to download files shared by a customer, but is receiving a message stating the site has been blocked. Which of the following is the MOST likely cause of this issue?
A. Antivirus software
B. Internet connectivity issues
C. Ransomware infection
D. Content-filtering
Correct Answer: D
Section: Soft Troubleshooting
Explanation
Explanation/Reference:

QUESTION 57
Joe, an end-user, reports that the PC he uses periodically logs off his user account and displays a message that updates are being installed. Which of the following is the MOST likely cause of this issue?
A. Time of day restrictions are enabled on the machine
B. Scheduled antivirus scans and updates are enabled on the machine
C. Remote desktop is enabled and an administrator has logged into the machine
D. Automatic Windows Update is enabled on the machine
Correct Answer: D
Section: Soft Troubleshooting
Explanation
Explanation/Reference:

QUESTION 58
A user advises that a computer is displaying pop-ups when connected to the Internet. After updating and running anti-malware software, the problem persists and the technician finds that two rogue processes cannot be killed. Which of the following should be done NEXT to continue troubleshooting the problem?
A. Run msconfig to clean boot the computer
B. Run Event Viewer to identify the cause
C. Run System Restore to revert to previous state
D. Run Recovery Console to kill the processes
Correct Answer: A
Section: Soft Troubleshooting
Explanation
Explanation/Reference:

QUESTION 59
A user reports that any URL entered redirects to the same web page. A technician concludes that the user's computer has been compromised. Which of the following tools would the technician use to resolve the issue?
A. Last known good configuration
B. Anti-malware
C. System restore
D. Rogue antivirus
Correct Answer: B
Section: Soft Troubleshooting
Explanation
Explanation/Reference:

QUESTION 60
A user's email inbox is suddenly receiving dozens of rejection messages from various mail servers. Which of the following would the technician perform to BEST solve the issue?

A. Change the user's email password.
B. Enable spam filtering on the email account.
C. Change the email account from POP to IMAP.
D. Disable the user's email account.
Correct Answer: A
Section: Soft Troubleshooting
Explanation
Explanation/Reference:

QUESTION 61
A technician receives a helpdesk ticket about an employee having a problem sending text messages with a company Android smartphone. It has been determined that it is not a carrier issue. Which of the following should the technician perform FIRST?
A. Verify data connectivity
B. Reformat the MicroSD card
C. Replace the SIM card
D. Perform a soft restore
Correct Answer: A
Section: Soft Troubleshooting
Explanation
Explanation/Reference:

QUESTION 62
A networked PC has started to display adware pop-ups when the user opens the browser. Which of the following best practices should the technician employ FIRST when responding to the problem?
A. Disable System Restore
B. Schedule scans and run updates in safe mode
C. Quarantine the system
D. Create a System Restore point
Correct Answer: C
Section: Soft Troubleshooting

Explanation
Explanation/Reference:

QUESTION 63
Joe, a user, states he is unable to use his Android phone after updating the OS. Joe is in a hurry and would like a quick solution that would most likely fix the issue. Which of the following methods can the technician use?
A. Initiate a factory reset
B. Perform a hard reset
C. Remove the MicroSD card
D. Rollback the OS update
Correct Answer: B
Section: Soft Troubleshooting
Explanation

Explanation/Reference:
QUESTION 64
A customer reports that a smartphone is experiencing a very short battery life. The user has been using this phone for a short time and has installed several apps recently. Which of the following might be the cause of the issue?
A. Slow data speeds
B. Defective SD card
C. Unauthorized root access
D. Signal drop or weak signal
Correct Answer: C
Section: Soft Troubleshooting
Explanation
Explanation/Reference:

QUESTION 65
A customer has recently installed several applications on a Windows 7

workstation and is now experiencing slow system performance and spontaneous restarts.
After removing some of the recently installed applications, the issue persists. Which of the following tools could the technician use to troubleshoot the problem while preventing data loss?
A. Factory restore
B. SecureBoot
C. msconfig
D. diskpart
Correct Answer: C
Section: Soft Troubleshooting
Explanation
Explanation/Reference:

QUESTION 66
A user's smartphone runs very slow at the end of the day. When the user restarts the phone in the morning, it runs at its normal speed. Which of the following should be done throughout the day to BEST resolve this issue?
A. Reset to the smartphone to factory default.
B. Uninstall any unused apps.
C. Close all running apps.
D. Charge the smartphone.
Correct Answer: C
Section: Soft Troubleshooting
Explanation
Explanation/Reference:

QUESTION 67
After installing a critical update from Windows Update, a user accidentally types an incorrect URL into the browser and malware is automatically installed. The malware disables the computer's antivirus software and Internet connection. Which of the following would be the

BEST tool to remove the malware without risking loss of the user's data?
A. Run System Restore
B. Reinstall Windows with the Repair Option
C. Reinstall Windows on top of itself
D. Run System File Checker
Correct Answer: A
Section: Soft Troubleshooting
Explanation
Explanation/Reference:

QUESTION 68
Joe, a user, is using his smartphone for navigation while driving. As he drives, an icon frequently appears on the screen informing the user additional information is required to log in. Which of the following is causing this?
A. Unintended WiFi connections
B. Cellular data roaming notifications
C. Weak cellular signal
D. Unintended Bluetooth connections
Correct Answer: A
Section: Soft Troubleshooting
Explanation
Explanation/Reference:

QUESTION 69
An engineer working with large detailed CAD files notices over time that the workstation is taking significantly longer to open files that used to launch quickly. Other applications work fine, and the engineer confirms all of the data has been backed up the night before. A technician determines that the workstation is about two years old. Which of the following would be the technician's FIRST step in troubleshooting the problem?

A. Run defrag on the hard drive
B. Restore the CAD files from backup
C. Replace the hard drive
D. Remove and reinstall the CAD software
Correct Answer: A
Section: Soft Troubleshooting
Explanation
Explanation/Reference:

QUESTION 70
Joe, an end-user, reports that the Windows PC he is using automatically locks when he leaves his desk and walks to a printer to retrieve documents. Joe is then required to type in his username and password to unlock the computer. The technician looks at the settings on the PC and notices that the screensaver and screen-lock options are grayed out on the computer and cannot be changed. Which of the following is the MOST likely cause of this issue?
A. Domain-level group policies
B. Antivirus domain-level policies
C. Corrupted registry settings
D. Incorrect local-level user policies
Correct Answer: A
Section: Soft Troubleshooting
Explanation
Explanation/Reference:

QUESTION 71
A Windows workstation is suspected of having malicious software that created an infected start-up item or service. Which of the following tools would a technician use to test this theory?
A. chkdsk
B. msconfig
C. dxdiag

D. ipconfig
Correct Answer: B
Section: Soft Troubleshooting
Explanation
Explanation/Reference:

QUESTION 72
A user reports unexpected icons appearing on the desktop. The technician identifies that the symptoms point to a malware infection. Which of the following procedures would be performed NEXT?
A. Quarantine infected system
B. Schedule scans and run updates
C. Report the issue to the information security officer
D. Disable System Restore (in Windows)
E. Educate end user
Correct Answer: A
Section: Soft Troubleshooting
Explanation
Explanation/Reference:

QUESTION 73
A user updates the video driver on the computer and it requests a restart after installation. The computer never gets past the loading Windows page without rebooting. Which of the following should the technician use to resolve this issue without losing any vital files or programs?
A. Emergency Repair Disk
B. Restore from OEM image
C. System Recovery
D. Restore from backup
Correct Answer: C
Section: Soft Troubleshooting

Explanation
Explanation/Reference:

QUESTION 74
A user is having issues with a Windows computer. Upon loading the operating system, several messages appear referring to a DLL file that cannot be found. Which of the following would be the BEST course of action for the technician to perform NEXT?
A. Copy the DLL file from a working PC and use the regsvr32 command to load the file
B. Run the Windows Update utility to manually reinstall the DLL file
C. Run the defrag utility to correct any fragmentation that may have damaged the file
D. Research the DLL file to identify the application it corresponds to before continuing
Correct Answer: D
Section: Soft Troubleshooting
Explanation
Explanation/Reference:

QUESTION 75
A user, Ann, receives a phone call from the company's mail administrator who indicates her email account has been disabled due to high volumes of emails being sent in a very short period of time. Which of the following types of attack has the user experienced?
A. Virus infection
B. Man-in-the-middle attack
C. Phishing attack
D. Malware infection
Correct Answer: A
Section: Soft Troubleshooting

Explanation
Explanation/Reference:

QUESTION 76
A mobile phone has started to respond slowly and erratically. The user has done a soft reset and the problem still exists. Which of the following is the BEST step the user can take to fix this problem?
A. Perform a force stop
B. Reset to factory default
C. Upgrade to a larger battery
D. Close running apps
Correct Answer: B
Section: Soft Troubleshooting
Explanation
Explanation/Reference:

QUESTION 77
A user reports browsing the Internet is slow and an icon with a picture of a person with a headset keeps asking them to "click here for help." The user has clicked on the icon to try to resolve the slowness but all that happens is the computer redirects them to a website to purchase software. Which of the following should be performed FIRST to resolve the issue?
A. Create a restore point
B. Run O/S updates
C. Train the user of malicious software
D. Identify the type of malware
Correct Answer: D
Section: Soft Troubleshooting
Explanation
Explanation/Reference:

QUESTION 78

A technician receives a call regarding a PC's slow performance. The client states that most applications are slow to respond; boot up and shutdown take much longer than they used to. Hard drive diagnostics pass, but there are error messages in the event viewer stating that the file system is corrupt. Which of the following should the technician do NEXT?
A. Reload the OS using FAT32 instead of NTFS.
B. Change the disk from basic to dynamic.
C. Run chkdsk with the /r switch and reboot the PC.
D. Open the defrag utility and run a drive analysis.
Correct Answer: C
Section: Soft Troubleshooting
Explanation
Explanation/Reference:

QUESTION 79
A technician has just fixed a user's PC and successfully removed a virus and malware from the machine. Which of the following is the LAST thing the technician should do?
A. Educate the user regarding Internet browsing best practices
B. Update the anti-malware software on the user's PC
C. Schedule scans and run updates
D. Enable system restore and create restore point
Correct Answer: A
Section: Soft Troubleshooting
Explanation
Explanation/Reference:

QUESTION 80
Ann, a user, states that after installing an update on her iPhone, the WiFi starts to malfunction. The WiFi icon is displaying that it has connectivity but she is still unable to browse. Which of the following could be the issue?

A. PRAM needs to be reset
B. iCloud is corrupted
C. The router needs to be rebooted
D. The upgrade needs to be uninstalled
Correct Answer: A
Section: Soft Troubleshooting
Explanation
Explanation/Reference:

QUESTION 81
Joe, a user, returned yesterday from a trip where he utilized the GPS function of his mobile device. He now notices the battery is rapidly draining. Which of the following can Joe MOST likely do to resolve the issue without a loss of data?
A. Restart the mobile device.
B. Update the device's firmware.
C. Uninstall the GPS-enabled app.
D. Readjust the location settings.
Correct Answer: D
Section: Soft Troubleshooting
Explanation
Explanation/Reference:

QUESTION 82
Joe, a user, has connected a tablet to his personal mobile hotspot device in a public location for Internet access. The device display indicates there are two connections instead of just one. Which of the following actions can he perform to prevent this unauthorized access to the device immediately? (Select TWO).
A. Change the SSID to a different broadcast name
B. Add the intruding device to a blocked access list
C. Access the intruder's device and shut it down
D. Shut down the device until the intruder is no longer in the area

E. Set up a WiFi analyzer to identify the intruding device
Correct Answer: AB
Section: Soft Troubleshooting
Explanation
Explanation/Reference:

QUESTION 83
Ann, a customer, reports that when she occasionally works in the office basement, her smartphone battery drains faster than normal and she has poor cellular reception. Which of the following is the reason for the fast battery drain?
A. Unpaired Bluetooth
B. Weak signal
C. Defective SD card
D. Malware
Correct Answer: B
Section: Soft Troubleshooting
Explanation
Explanation/Reference:

QUESTION 84
A technician suspects that a computer issue is caused by a failed NIC. Following the troubleshooting theory, which of the following is the NEXT step the technician
should take?
A. Identify the problem
B. Document findings, actions and outcome
C. Verify full system functionality
D. Establish a theory of probable cause
E. Test the theory to determine cause
Correct Answer: E
Section: Op Procedure

Explanation
Explanation/Reference:

QUESTION 85
A new help desk technician receives a trouble call from a user. The issue is something the technician has never encountered before, and does not know where to begin troubleshooting. The FIRST course of action is for the technician to:
A. tell the customer the issue needs to be escalated to a higher tier technician.
B. ask the customer if they would mind holding for no more than two minutes to check resources.
C. tell the customer this is the first time encountering the issue and to please be patient.
D. ask the customer to please hold while a senior technician is consulted regarding the issue.
Correct Answer: B
Section: Op Procedure
Explanation
Explanation/Reference:

QUESTION 86
A technician is working on a home theater PC in a location where the electrical system may not be properly grounded. As the technician is finishing the installation, which of the following should the computer technician do before connecting a cable TV line to a TV tuner card?
A. Perform self-grounding
B. Unplug the computer power cable
C. Use an ESD strap
D. Require the electrical system be brought up to code
Correct Answer: B
Section: Op Procedure

Explanation
Explanation/Reference:

QUESTION 87
When dealing with a difficult customer, which of the following is the BEST way to handle the situation?
A. Do not argue with the customer and/or be defensive
B. Use technical terms to assure customer confidence
C. Escalate the customer's issue to a supervisor
D. Sympathize with the customer about issue
Correct Answer: A
Section: Op Procedure

Explanation
Explanation/Reference:

QUESTION 88
A technician troubleshooting a computer finds a faulty video card and needs to replace it. Which of the following safety procedures should be used to prevent damaging the new part?
A. Ground the computer and remove jewelry.
B. Self ground and handle the new card by the edges.
C. Place the computer on an ESD mat.
D. Attach an ESD strap to the new card during handling.
Correct Answer: B
Section: Op Procedure
Explanation
Explanation/Reference:

QUESTION 89
A technician opens a customer's computer and sees large amounts of accumulated dust. Which of the following is the BEST method of removing the dust from the computer?

A. Use compressed air to free the dust from the components and remove it with an ESD vacuum.
B. Dampen an ESD cloth with denatured alcohol and use it to gently wipe the dust away.
C. Use a shop vacuum with enough power to ensure all dust has been removed.
D. Remove as much dust as possible by hand and use compressed air to blow the rest out.
Correct Answer: A

QUESTION 90
Which of the following protocols would be used for file sharing between MAC OS and Windows OS workstations on a LAN?
A. IMAP
B. SMB
C. SSH
D. RDP
Correct Answer: B
Section: Hardware
Explanation
Explanation/Reference:

QUESTION 91
Which of the following Internet connection types is known to have a significantly higher latency than the others?
A. Cable
B. Satellite
C. DSL
D. Fiber
Correct Answer: B
Section: Hardware
Explanation
Explanation/Reference:

QUESTION 92
Under normal circumstances, which of the following wireless standards provides the slowest transfer speed at 2.4GHz?
A. 802.11a
B. 802.11b
C. 802.11g
D. 802.11n
Correct Answer: B
Section: Hardware
Explanation
Explanation/Reference:

QUESTION 93
An IT Director wants to increase security on the company website to prevent man-in-the-middle attacks. Which of the following Internet protocols should be implemented to meet the requirement?
A. HTTPS
B. IMAP
C. TELNET
D. SMTP
Correct Answer: A
Section: Hardware
Explanation
Explanation/Reference:

QUESTION 94
Which of the following ports is used for a secure browser connection for an online purchase?
A. 23
B. 80
C. 110
D. 443
E. 3389

Correct Answer: D
Section: Networking
Explanation
Explanation/Reference:

QUESTION 95
Which of the following ports is typically used for sending email?
A. 21
B. 22
C. 23
D. 25
Correct Answer: D
Section: Networking
Explanation
Explanation/Reference:

QUESTION 96
Which of the following connectors are commonly used for fiber optic cables?
A. RJ-11 and RJ-45
B. ST and LC
C. F-connectors
D. BNC
Correct Answer: B
Section: Networking
Explanation
Explanation/Reference:

QUESTION 97
A machine receives an IP address starting with 169.254.x.x when which of the following occurs?
A. When the machine is using IPv6
B. When the next IP range begins with 169.253
C. When the DHCP server does not respond
D. When the operating system is Unix or Linux

Correct Answer: C
Section: Networking
Explanation
Explanation/Reference:

QUESTION 98
A technician is connecting a PoE enabled phone and needs to run the drop from the switch that is 55 meters (180.4 feet) away. Which of the following cable types would be the MOST suitable for this purpose?
A. Fiber
B. Coaxial
C. CAT3
D. CAT6
Correct Answer: D
Section: Networking
Explanation
Explanation/Reference:

QUESTION 99
Which of the following is an advantage of using DHCP for network addressing?
A. Simplified configuration
B. More addresses are available
C. Faster connection speeds
D. Lower latency times
Correct Answer: A
Section: Networking
Explanation
Explanation/Reference:

QUESTION 100
A user wants to implement a wireless router that will have the fastest data speeds and operate over the 5GHz frequency. Which of the following standards should the user select?

A. 802.11a
B. 802.11ac
C. 802.11g
D. 802.11n
Correct Answer: B
Section: Networking
Explanation
Explanation/Reference:

QUESTION 101
Which of the following devices is BEST to use when designing a SOHO network to ensure the least amount of collisions?
A. Switch
B. Bridge
C. Hub
D. Access point
Correct Answer: A
Section: Networking
Explanation
Explanation/Reference:

QUESTION 102
Which of the following Internet connection types is a digital form that runs over standard telephone wiring?
A. Fiber
B. Dial-up
C. Cable
D. DSL
Correct Answer: D
Section: Networking
Explanation
Explanation/Reference:

QUESTION 103
The device that allows two different networks to communicate

with one another is:
A. a repeater.
B. a hub.
C. a router.
D. an access point.
Correct Answer: C
Section: Networking
Explanation
Explanation/Reference:

QUESTION 104
A technician is tasked with finding and labeling where a network connection terminates in a patch panel. Which of the following tools would be BEST for the
technician to use?
A. Ethernet cable tester
B. Tone generator and probe
C. RJ-45 loopback plug
D. Patch panel punchdown tool
Correct Answer: B
Section: Networking
Explanation
Explanation/Reference:

QUESTION 105
A technician is tasked with replacing all the APs in an office building for greater speeds. The current location of APs allowed for total coverage of WiFi throughout the office. Which of the following 802.11 standards should be used?
A. a
B. ac
C. b
D. g
E. n
Correct Answer: B

Section: Networking
Explanation
Explanation/Reference:

QUESTION 106
Joe, a technician, is tasked to install a new client machine. He notices the machine is not getting any network connectivity. He tests the network cable between the PC and the network jack and confirms it is good. Joe goes to the network closet and finds several network cables not connected to the switch. Which of the following tools would Joe use to determine which cable goes back to the correct network jack?
A. Loopback plug
B. Toner probe
C. WiFi analyzer
D. Punchdown tool
Correct Answer: B
Section: Networking
Explanation
Explanation/Reference:

QUESTION 107
A network administrator has a requirement to implement a WiFi hotspot for the public. Which of the following should be used for secure access?
A. WEP and TKIP
B. WPA2 and AES
C. WPA and static IPs
D. WPA2 and MAC filtering
Correct Answer: B
Section: Networking
Explanation
Explanation/Reference:

QUESTION 108

Which of the following is a public IP address?
A. 10.45.xxx.xxx
B. 169.254.xxx.xxx
C. 173.16.xxx.xxx
D. 192.168.xxx.xxx
Correct Answer: C
Section: Networking
Explanation
Explanation/Reference:

QUESTION 109
A technician needs to run a cable for a new computer and the requirement is CAT6. Which of the following wiring connectors should the technician use when
terminating the cable?
A. BNC
B. RJ-12
C. RJ-45
D. ST
E. F-connector
Correct Answer: C
Section: Networking
Explanation
Explanation/Reference:

QUESTION 110
Which of the following BEST describes the reason a network administrator would task a technician with replacing a hub with a switch?
A. The hub did not provide PoE
B. The hub had too many collisions
C. The hub was out of ports
D. The hub had a bad port
Correct Answer: B
Section: Networking

Explanation
Explanation/Reference:

QUESTION 111
There are 20 laptops in a room and they all need to connect wirelessly to the network. Which of the following would be the BEST device to use?
A. Switch
B. Router
C. Access point
D. Hub
Correct Answer: C
Section: Networking
Explanation
Explanation/Reference:

QUESTION 112
A user wants to quickly share pictures between mobile devices. The devices will be in close proximity so the necessity of a third party service and/or another networking device is not required. Which of the following is the BEST option for this scenario?
A. NFC
B. USB
C. IR
D. WiFi
Correct Answer: A
Section: Mobile Devices
Explanation
Explanation/Reference:

QUESTION 113
Which of the following would need to be enabled on a mobile phone to share its Internet connection with multiple devices simultaneously?
A. NFC
B. Bluetooth

C. Hotspot
D. Tethering
Correct Answer: C
Section: Mobile Devices
Explanation
Explanation/Reference:

QUESTION 114
Android smartphones are typically different from other smartphone devices in that:

A. Android devices use apps that are more secure than other devices.
B. Android devices use open source operating systems.
C. Android devices can only operate with a proprietary operating system.
D. Android devices can receive apps from different sources.
Correct Answer: B
Section: Mobile Devices
Explanation
Explanation/Reference:

QUESTION 115
Recently a company updated their network infrastructure. A user reports that a laptop is experiencing slower network speeds since the update. Which of the following would the technician replace, rather than purchase a new device?
A. Wireless NIC
B. CPU
C. RAM
D. Hard drive
Correct Answer: A
Section: Mobile Devices
Explanation
Explanation/Reference:

QUESTION 116
Legacy software needs to be installed on a netbook. Which of the following is MOST likely needed in order to install the software?
A. Lightning port
B. Bluetooth adapter
C. USB optical drive
D. NFC chip
Correct Answer: C
Section: Mobile Devices
Explanation
Explanation/Reference:

QUESTION 117
Wearable fitness tracking devices use which of the following technologies to determine user activity levels?
A. Digitizer
B. Gyroscope
C. Accelerometer
D. Inverter
Correct Answer: C
Section: Mobile Devices
Explanation
Explanation/Reference:

QUESTION 118
A user, Ann, is preparing to travel abroad and wants to ensure that her laptop will work properly. Which of the following components of the laptop should be verified FIRST to ensure power compatibility before traveling?
A. Wall adapter
B. Battery
C. Power supply
D. Digitizer
Correct Answer: A
Section: Mobile Devices

Explanation
Explanation/Reference:

QUESTION 119
A laptop is setup at a podium for a presentation but is set to extended desktop. The presenter would like it to show exactly what the laptop screen is showing.
Which of the following would be the QUICKEST way to accomplish this?
A. Look for the setting in control panel
B. Toggle the dual display function key
C. Change the screen orientation
D. Reboot the laptop
Correct Answer: B
Section: Mobile Devices
Explanation
Explanation/Reference:

QUESTION 120
A laptop has a network port that is not working consistently and wireless is out of range. Which of the following would the technician do to quickly get the laptop back on the wired network?
A. Use a USB to RJ-45 dongle
B. Enable Bluetooth
C. Enable NIC teaming
D. Replace the motherboard
Correct Answer: A
Section: Mobile Devices
Explanation
Explanation/Reference:

QUESTION 121
A customer wants the thinnest laptop possible. Which of the following display technologies typically allows for thinner devices?

A. IPS
B. OLED
C. LCD
D. DisplayPort
Correct Answer: B
Section: Mobile Devices
Explanation
Explanation/Reference:

QUESTION 122
Which of the following components is responsible for converting light into digital information?
A. Microphone
B. Digitizer
C. Inverter
D. Webcam
Correct Answer: D
Section: Mobile Devices
Explanation
Explanation/Reference:

QUESTION 123
A customer brings a laptop in for repair, because the screen image is upside down. Which of the following is the BEST solution?

A. Change the screen orientation
B. Replace the video card
C. Connect an external monitor
D. Update the video card drivers
Correct Answer: A
Section: Mobile Devices
Explanation
Explanation/Reference:

QUESTION 124
A user is requesting a cable to charge and transfer data for an Apple mobile device. Which of the following connection types would satisfy the user's requirements?
A. MicroUSB
B. Molex
C. MiniUSB
D. Lightning
Correct Answer: D
Section: Mobile Devices
Explanation
Explanation/Reference:

QUESTION 125
A user reports that the cursor jumps to random screen locations when typing on a laptop computer. Which of the following devices is MOST likely causing this?
A. The touchpad
B. The mouse wheel
C. The multimedia keys
D. The digitizer
Correct Answer: A
Section: Mobile Devices
Explanation
Explanation/Reference:

QUESTION 126
A user has requested a device that could be used for web-conferences while away from work. The device will mainly be used for emailing, document reviewing, and phone calls. Which of the following mobile devices would a technician MOST likely recommend?
A. Tablet
B. Smart camera
C. Phablet

D. Web camera
Correct Answer: C
Section: Mobile Devices
Explanation
Explanation/Reference:

QUESTION 127
A customer struggles with the small print of most smartphones. The customer still likes the idea of using a smartphone for phone calls and work. Which of the following devices should the technician recommend to the customer?
A. A tablet
B. An e-Reader
C. A phablet
D. A smart watch
Correct Answer: C
Section: Mobile Devices
Explanation
Explanation/Reference:

QUESTION 128
A user has downloaded an image file and needs to install an application from the image. When trying to execute or open the file, an error is displayed. Which of the following should the user perform?
A. Download a different file from the website
B. Rename the extension of the file to a known extension
C. Verify the MD5 hash of the downloaded file
D. Mount the file as an emulated DVD
Correct Answer: D
Section: Mobile Devices
Explanation
Explanation/Reference:

QUESTION 129

A customer asks a technician for a device that has the capability to easily connect a laptop to an external monitor, keyboard, mouse, and charge the battery. Which of the following devices should the technician recommend to the customer?
A. Lightning
B. KVM switch
C. USB 3.0
D. Docking station
Correct Answer: D
Section: Mobile Devices
Explanation
Explanation/Reference:

QUESTION 130
A technician is working on a laptop with a failed Ethernet port caused by ESD. Which of the following is the simplest solution to restore network connectivity?
A. Re-solder the network connector
B. Replace the Ethernet daughter board
C. Update the Ethernet driver
D. Enable wireless and connect to the WAP
Correct Answer: D
Section: Mobile Devices
Explanation
Explanation/Reference:

QUESTION 131
When a technician is planning to replace a laptop hard drive, the technician will need to:
A. select a drive that is the correct form factor.
B. choose the correct drive cache size for the laptop.
C. also upgrade the memory.
D. verify voltage requirements.
Correct Answer: A
Section: Mobile Devices

Explanation
Explanation/Reference:

QUESTION 132
A laptop logon screen can barely be seen, despite adjusting the display's brightness setting. Which of the following display components is defective?
A. Backlight
B. Digitizer
C. Inverter
D. Polarizer
Correct Answer: A
Section: Mobile Devices
Explanation
Explanation/Reference:

QUESTION 133
A network technician has been tasked with deploying new VoIP phones on a network. When the technician plugs the Ethernet cable for the phone into the wall port, the phone fails to turn on. When the technician plugs the Ethernet cable directly into the computer, the computer is able to access the network. Which of the following is the MOST likely cause of this issue?

A. The network switch does not support PoE
B. The technician is connecting the phone to the wrong type of port
C. The firewall on the network is blocking access to the DHCP server
D. The Ethernet cable is the wrong type
Correct Answer: A
Section: Hardware NetTroublshooting
Explanation
Explanation/Reference:

QUESTION 134
A technician cannot communicate with one particular IP address and needs to narrow down where the traffic is stopping. Which of the following commands would
be used to determine this?
A. nslookup
B. ipconfig
C. nbtstat
D. ping
E. tracert
Correct Answer: E
Section: Hardware & NetTroublshooting
Explanation
Explanation/Reference:

QUESTION 135
A user reports that a workstation fails to complete boot up and repeats a series of two beeps over and over. The user states that the workstation had been displaying BSOD errors after running multiple applications. Which of the following is the MOST likely cause?
A. Video adapter failure
B. Memory failure
C. Power supply failure
D. CPU failure
Correct Answer: B
Section: Hardware NetTroublshooting
Explanation
Explanation/Reference:

QUESTION 136
A technician is troubleshooting a desktop that is having intermittent issues with locking up and system errors. The technician suspects that the problem might be that not enough

power is getting to the motherboard. Which of the following tools would a technician use to determine if the hypothesis is correct?
A. POST card
B. Loopback plug
C. Multimeter
D. Cable tester
Correct Answer: C
Section: Hardware NetTroublshooting
Explanation
Explanation/Reference:

QUESTION 137
A user is notified of file system errors on an external hard drive. Which of the following tools can be used to repair common errors on the drive?
A. chkdsk
B. diskpart
C. format
D. sfc
Correct Answer: A
Section: Hardware NetTroublshooting
Explanation
Explanation/Reference:

QUESTION 138
A technician has upgraded the BIOS of a system that is running with multiple hard drives. Afterward, the system will not boot and displays an error message
"Operating system not found". Which of the following is the FIRST thing the technician should inspect?
A. The hard drive type settings in the BIOS
B. The power supply connections to the hard drives
C. The boot sequence settings in the BIOS
D. The motherboard SATA connectors
Correct Answer: C

Section: Hardware NetTroublshooting
Explanation
Explanation/Reference:

QUESTION 139
An office printer that was working earlier in the day is no longer printing any documents. Pre-existing workstations are manually configured to print to the printer directly over the network. A technician has started to troubleshoot the problem and determines that the printer can still be seen in the network directory. The technician has also verified that the printer can print self-diagnostic pages successfully. Which of the following is the MOST likely cause of the problem?
A. The printer's IP address has changed.
B. The network print spooler service has been restarted.
C. "Perform Printer Maintenance" message is displayed on the printer's LCD panel.
D. Two or more users sent print jobs simultaneously, causing a print collision.
Correct Answer: A
Section: Hardware NetTroublshooting
Explanation
Explanation/Reference:

QUESTION 140
A technician receives a call that a client's PC is not booting after a recent test of the building's back-up generators. When the technician arrives, it is discovered that, once powered on, there is no output display or POST beep codes. Furthermore, after 15 seconds, the system's fans begin running much louder and faster. Which of the following is the MOST likely issue?
A. The motherboard was damaged by the power test.
B. The PC's RAM was affected by ESD.
C. The power supply was damaged and is nonfunctional.
D. The hard drive was erased due to the power test.

Correct Answer: A
Section: Hardware NetTroublshooting
Explanation
Explanation/Reference:

QUESTION 141
A technician receives a report from a client that is having issues with colors on a monitor. The technician notices that the monitor does not appear to have any red hues. The technician sees that the monitor has two types of inputs, VGA is currently in use, and the HDMI cable is not. The technician powers down the system and switches from using the VGA cable to the HDMI cable and the issue is resolved. Which of the following was MOST likely the issue?
A. One of the pins on the VGA cable was damaged.
B. The monitor did not natively support VGA input.
C. The PC was originally configured to output to HDMI.
D. The video card drivers were out of date.
Correct Answer: A
Section: Hardware NetTroublshooting
Explanation
Explanation/Reference:

QUESTION 142
A client has an issue with large files taking a long time to open or save. As time goes by, the issue worsens. The client has hundreds of GBs of files that are still in the process of backing up. The technician has verified that the hard drive is healthy and there are no signs of failure. Which of the following troubleshooting steps should the technician perform NEXT?
A. Install the latest drivers from the hardware vendor.
B. Perform a scan of the drive for file fragmentation.
C. Run chkdsk on the workstation's hard drive.
D. Reformat the drive and reinstall the OS.
Correct Answer: B

Section: Hardware NetTroublshooting
Explanation
Explanation/Reference:

QUESTION 143
A client, Ann, is having issues with a PC shutting down. There are no error messages displayed before the system powers off. Ann reports that this started after she installed and began using CAD software. The hard drive, video card, and RAM all meet the software requirements and have passed diagnostics. Which of the following is MOST likely the issue?
A. The video card has 3D acceleration disabled.
B. The hard drive is IDE instead of SATA.
C. The hard drive needs to be repartitioned.
D. The PSU is underpowered for the system.
Correct Answer: D
Section: Hardware NetTroublshooting
Explanation
Explanation/Reference:

QUESTION 144
A printer on the second floor is not printing for anyone. However, the printer has power and displays ready on the LCD display. There is paper in the trays and the toner was recently changed. The system administrator goes to the location with a laptop and tests the network port and is able to connect. Jobs are being queued on the local machines. Which of the following should the system administrator do to get the printer functioning again?
A. Move the printer to a known good port and connect to the network
B. Replace the network cable to the printer
C. Verify the server's print spooler service is running
D. Attach the printer directly to the laptop and print a test page
Correct Answer: C

Section: Hardware NetTroublshooting
Explanation
Explanation/Reference:

QUESTION 145
The OSD of a monitor indicates the proper video source is selected, but no image is displayed. Which of the following issues are the MOST likely reasons? (Select TWO).
A. The source cable is disconnected
B. The monitor's brightness is set too low
C. The backlighting of the monitor is faulty
D. The monitor's contrast is set too high
E. No device is sending source video
Correct Answer: AE
Section: Hardware NetTroublshooting
Explanation
Explanation/Reference:

QUESTION 146
The loud clicking noise coming from a faulty hard drive is MOST likely created by:
A. the coil reversing polarity in an endless loop.
B. one or more bad spindle motor bearings.
C. repeated motion of the read/write head armature parallel to the platter.
D. the solid state read/write head scratching the platter surface.
Correct Answer: C
Section: Hardware NetTroublshooting
Explanation
Explanation/Reference:

QUESTION 147
A workstation has a network link light, but it cannot access internal network resources. Which of the following is the MOST likely cause of the issue?

A. Slow transfer speeds
B. IP address conflict
C. Incorrect gateway
D. Packet collisions
Correct Answer: B
Section: Hardware NetTroublshooting
Explanation
Explanation/Reference:

QUESTION 148
Joe, a technician, is preparing to replace a laptop screen. This laptop has a touch screen to support Windows 8.1 in order to use the Metro tiles. Which of the following is the FIRST step the technician should perform?
A. Remove the laptop bezel
B. Document and label each cable and screw location
C. Organize the replacement parts
D. Refer to the manufacturer's documentation
Correct Answer: D
Section: Hardware NetTroublshooting
Explanation
Explanation/Reference:

QUESTION 149
A user has reported that the company notebook is performing some random mouse actions requiring the user to make a lot of typing corrections. How can the technician solve the issue for the user?
A. Adjust the mouse settings so the mouse moves slower
B. Reverse the buttons on the mouse pad
C. Adjust the mouse settings so the mouse moves faster
D. Use the function keys to disable the mouse pad
Correct Answer: D
Section: Hardware NetTroublshooting
Explanation

Explanation/Reference:

QUESTION 150
A network printer is online and ready. The accounting group is unable to print to this network printer, but other departments can. Which of the following would the technician use to resolve the problem?
A. Replace the printer's network cable
B. Modify the security setting of the print spooler
C. Restart the TCP/IP print spooler service
D. Use the manufacturer's maintenance kit
Correct Answer: B
Section: Hardware NetTroublshooting
Explanation
Explanation/Reference:

QUESTION 151
A customer has left a computer monitor on over the weekend and now notices slight discoloration of the screen. This is an example of:
A. a failing backlight.
B. burn in.
C. a bad inverter.
D. dead pixels.
E. EMI.
Correct Answer: B
Section: Hardware NetTroublshooting
Explanation
Explanation/Reference:

QUESTION 152
A user, Ann, reports that her company laptop cannot pick up a wireless connection in certain areas of a building. However, users working on their laptops in the common areas have Internet connectivity. Which of the following is the MOST likely cause?

A. Weak RF signals
B. Out of date Ethernet driver
C. Enabled MAC filtering
D. Duplicate IP addresses
Correct Answer: A
Section: Hardware NetTroublshooting
Explanation
Explanation/Reference:

QUESTION 153
After receiving a call from an executive, a technician walks into a meeting room to find that the projector is not showing the screen of the executive's laptop. The projector shows a message that reads "No video signal". Which of the following is the FIRST thing that the technician should do?
A. Adjust the laptop's screen brightness
B. Replace the projector's bulb
C. Verify the VGA cable is connected
D. Ensure secondary display is enabled
Correct Answer: C
Section: Hardware NetTroublshooting
Explanation
Explanation/Reference:

QUESTION 154
A user states there are multiple small black dots on an LCD screen. Which of the following should be done to resolve the issue?
A. Replace monitor.
B. Replace video card.
C. Replace video cable.
D. Replace power supply.
Correct Answer: A
Section: Hardware NetTroublshooting
Explanation

Explanation/Reference:

QUESTION 155
A client's computer is not connecting to a website. Which of the following commands will allow the technician to view the route/number of hops between the host and remote systems?
A. nbtstat
B. tracert
C. nslookup
D. netstat
Correct Answer: B
Section: Hardware NetTroublshooting
Explanation
Explanation/Reference:

QUESTION 156
A user is trying to use an external hard drive with an incompatible file system. Which of the following tools will allow the user to change the file system on the hard drive?
A. format
B. defrag
C. bootrec
D. chkdsk
Correct Answer: A
Section: Hardware NetTroublshooting
Explanation
Explanation/Reference:

QUESTION 157
A brownout has occurred within a building. A technician is repairing a workstation which has a power light, but is not displaying anything on the screen and is not making any sounds during boot up. Which of the following should be used to further troubleshoot the workstation?

A. Loop back plug
B. POST card
C. Power supply tester
D. Multimeter
Correct Answer: B
Section: Hardware NetTroublshooting
Explanation
Explanation/Reference:

QUESTION 158
A user is reporting that a desktop monitor backlighting is very dim. Which of the following should be performed FIRST when troubleshooting the problem?
A. Update drivers
B. Reseat the video card
C. Use OSD tools
D. Replace the monitor
Correct Answer: C
Section: Hardware NetTroublshooting
Explanation
Explanation/Reference:

QUESTION 159
A user reports that the mouse is not working properly. The technician notices on the user's workstation that the mouse cursor spins for several minutes before the technician can use the mouse. Which of the following is the cause of the issue?

A. Failed Operating System
B. Faulty mouse
C. Faulty CPU
D. Not enough memory
Correct Answer: D
Section: Hardware NetTroublshooting

Explanation
Explanation/Reference:

QUESTION 160
A technician replaces a failed hard drive with a brand new one. The technician boots from a PE CD and attempts to install a custom OS build deployed from the network. The hard drive is visible in the system's BIOS. However, once in the preinstallation environment, the drive is not recognized in the imaging process and the process fails. Which of the following is MOST likely the cause of failure?
A. The boot CD has failed and needs to be replaced.
B. The hard drive needs to have its configuration manually defined in the BIOS.
C. The PC's power supply is not providing enough power to the new hard drive.
D. The hard drive has not been partitioned correctly.
Correct Answer: D
Section: Hardware NetTroublshooting
Explanation
Explanation/Reference:

QUESTION 161
A technician is notified that a laptop is not booting. It is discovered that there are no system lights, sounds, or display when the power button is pressed. Which of the following should the technician attempt FIRST in the troubleshooting process?
A. Connect an external monitor into the laptop to determine if the LCD has failed.
B. Boot the system from either a boot CD or other removable media type.
C. Disconnect the AC and battery power and hold the power button for several seconds.
D. Remove any hard drives or optical drives, RAM, and any wireless cards or USB devices from the laptop.

Correct Answer: C
Section: Hardware NetTroublshooting
Explanation
Explanation/Reference:

QUESTION 162
A user attempts to turn on a computer and receives no response. The user calls the technician to report the computer is not booting and a faint smell of something burning. Which of the following tools will BEST help to identify the issue?
A. ESD strap
B. PSU tester
C. Cable tester
D. Loopback plug
Correct Answer: B
Section: Hardware NetTroublshooting
Explanation
Explanation/Reference:

QUESTION 163
A user notices the printer that is used for printing global shipper's labels is missing columns in the printed labels. The special label stock is new and appears to be fine. Which of the following should the technician perform FIRST when troubleshooting this problem?
A. Remove any stuck labels from the paper path
B. Clean the pickup rollers and check them for wear
C. Clean the print head with approved materials
D. Replace and realign the print head
Correct Answer: C
Section: Hardware NetTroublshooting
Explanation
Explanation/Reference:

QUESTION 164

Ann, a user, reports her docked mobile workstation will periodically lose her network share drive and lose video to the second monitor. Which of the following is
MOST likely the cause of this anomaly?
A. The workstation battery needs to be replaced.
B. The NIC is functioning intermittently.
C. Failed driver updates for the workstation's devices.
D. The surge protector lost AC power.
Correct Answer: D
Section: Hardware NetTroublshooting
Explanation
Explanation/Reference:

QUESTION 165
A user reports an inkjet printer is constantly feeding two sheets of paper for every page printed. Which of the following is the MOST likely reason?
A. Poor paper quality
B. Incorrect paper size
C. Defective duplexer
D. Worn feed rollers
Correct Answer: D
Section: Hardware NetTroublshooting
Explanation
Explanation/Reference:

QUESTION 166
A technician is working on a server with high latency on the mapped network drive. Upon entry into the server room, the technician suspects an issue with one of the drives in the array. Which of the following would the technician do to resolve the problem?
A. Reseat the drive cable in the array.
B. Replace the RAID controller.
C. Replace the faulty drive in the array.

D. Reinstall the RAID drivers.
Correct Answer: C
Section: Hardware NetTroublshooting
Explanation
Explanation/Reference:

QUESTION 167
Joe, a user, receives a wireless router from his ISP with a pre-set password and configuration. He can connect to the router fine via Ethernet but cannot see the wireless signal on any of his devices. The LEDs on the router indicate that a wireless signal is broadcasting. Which of the following settings on the router does Joe need to adjust to enable the devices to see the wireless signal?
A. DHCP
B. IPv6
C. DMZ
D. SSID
Correct Answer: D
Section: Hardware NetTroublshooting
Explanation
Explanation/Reference:

QUESTION 168
A technician is tasked with upgrading the hard drives of a high-end workstation to SSD. The drives must be configured in a RAID array, but the RAID card does not support SSD. Which of the following would the technician verify in order to use the new drives?
A. Controller firmware
B. Power requirements
C. File system type
D. System BIOS
Correct Answer: A

Section: Hardware NetTroublshooting
Explanation

Explanation/Reference:

QUESTION 169
A customer states that when booting up the workstation, there is a message that says "no operating system detected"; then, it continues to boot into the operating system. The customer is preparing to modify files on a USB drive. Which of the following should a technician perform to resolve the problem?
A. Reinstall the operating system to reinstall the hardware drivers.
B. Modify the boot.ini within the operating system.
C. Modify the boot sequence within the UEFI.
D. Disable the TPM chip to turn off data encryption.
Correct Answer: C
Section: Mix Questions
Explanation
Explanation/Reference:

QUESTION 170
A customer signed up for the mobile pay service to use with their first generation smartphone but it does not work at any place that supports the mobile pay service.
Which of the following is missing from the customer's smartphone?
A. RFID
B. IMSI
C. NFC chip
D. Bluetooth
Correct Answer: C
Section: Mix Questions
Explanation
Explanation/Reference:
QUESTION 171

A user wants to store a personal video to view at a later time. Which of the following types of media is the LEAST expensive with a maximum capacity of 750MB?
A. USB drive
B. DVD-R
C. Blu-Ray
D. CD-R
Correct Answer: D
Section: Mix Questions
Explanation
Explanation/Reference:

QUESTION 172
A technician is building a workstation that will only be used to connect remotely to a server. Which of the following types of PC configurations is BEST suited for this
task?
A. Thin client
B. Home server PC
C. CAD workstation
D. AV workstation
Correct Answer: A
Section: Mix Questions
Explanation
Explanation/Reference:

QUESTION 173
A user is watching streaming video on a home network, but experiences buffering and delays when there are too many people on the network. Which of the
following is MOST likely to resolve the issue?
A. Disable SSID broadcast
B. Setup UPnP
C. Enable QoS
D. Configure DMZ

Correct Answer: C
Section: Mix Questions
Explanation
Explanation/Reference:

QUESTION 174
A small office would like to offer Internet access to customers while onsite. However, customers should not be able to access any corporate data. Which of the following networking features would BEST enable this?
A. Configure a guest wireless network
B. Implement a DMZ
C. Disable NAT on the wireless network
D. Disable the SSID
E. Assign static IPs for all devices
Correct Answer: A
Section: Mix Questions
Explanation
Explanation/Reference:

QUESTION 175
Which of the following types of media connectors carries digital video as well as audio?
A. DVI-D
B. DVI-A
C. HDMI
D. VGA
Correct Answer: C
Section: Mix Questions
Explanation
Explanation/Reference:

QUESTION 176
Which of the following is a type of fiber connector?

A. RJ-11
B. F-connector
C. BNC
D. ST
Correct Answer: D
Section: Mix Questions
Explanation
Explanation/Reference:

QUESTION 177
Which of the following ports is used when accessing a website with SSL encryption?
A. 22
B. 80
C. 110
D. 443
Correct Answer: D
Section: Mix Questions
Explanation
Explanation/Reference:

QUESTION 178
Which of the following monitor technologies provide the widest viewing angle with rich colors and consistent backlighting? (Select TWO).
A. Light Emitting Diode
B. In-Plane Switching
C. Plasma
D. Twisted Nematic
E. Cold Cathode Fluorescent Lamp
Correct Answer: AB
Section: Mix Questions
Explanation
Explanation/Reference:

QUESTION 179
A user wants to enable hands-free for a smartphone in a car. Which of the following needs to be performed?
A. Enable WiFi
B. Driver installation
C. Device pairing
D. Enable NFC
Correct Answer: C
Section: Mix Questions
Explanation
Explanation/Reference:

QUESTION 180
A client, Joe, has reported issues with the back cover of his company-issued smartphone. Joe stated that it seems to either come off on its own, or will not seat properly on the phone. Which of the following is MOST likely the problem?
A. The MicroSD card is not installed properly.
B. The battery needs to be replaced.
C. The charging port is bent.
D. The smartphone has a non-OEM cover.
Correct Answer: B
Section: Mix Questions
Explanation
Explanation/Reference:

QUESTION 181
A customer wants to copy a database that is 97GB in size for multiple uses. Which of the following format specifications should the customer use?

A. BD – RE DL
B. BDXL
C. BD – RE

D. BD-R
Correct Answer: A
Section: Mix Questions
Explanation
Explanation/Reference:

QUESTION 182
A technician is installing a wireless router to be used as an access point. The company firewall will assign IP addresses to devices on the wireless network. Which of the following settings does the technician need to disable on the wireless router to accomplish this?
A. NAT
B. DMZ
C. PAT
D. DHCP
Correct Answer: D
Section: Mix Questions
Explanation
Explanation/Reference:

QUESTION 183
Two drives in a RAID 5 have failed. Which of the following will the technician need to implement?
A. Replace the failed drives and restore the data from backup to the RAID.
B. Replace one of the failed drives and run the RAID repair.
C. Replace the failed drives and format the RAID using the quick option.
D. Replace one of the failed drives and repair the RAID using system utilities.
Correct Answer: A
Section: Mix Questions

Explanation
Explanation/Reference:

QUESTION 184
A user is unable to show an Android smartphone display on a TV. Which of the following settings should the technician check to resolve this issue?
A. Multi-window
B. Air view
C. Air browse
D. Screen mirroring
Correct Answer: D
Section: Mix Questions
Explanation
Explanation/Reference:

QUESTION 185
A network technician connects a tone generator to an RJ-45 drop. Which of the following is the MOST likely reason for doing this?
A. To validate proper wiring of the network jack
B. To confirm continuity of the conductors
C. To locate the position of the cable on a patch panel
D. To test the transmission quality of the connection
Correct Answer: C
Section: Mix Questions
Explanation
Explanation/Reference:

QUESTION 186
A SOHO is considering a purchase of several printers that will facilitate printing on both sides of the media. Which of the following optional add-ons will provide this functionality?

A. Collate

B. Duplex
C. Fast draft
D. Paper type
Correct Answer: B
Section: Mix Questions
Explanation
Explanation/Reference:

QUESTION 187
A group of users need to connect directly to a printer with continuous access. Which of the following connection types will achieve this?
A. Serial
B. Ethernet
C. USB
D. eSATA
Correct Answer: B